How to Benefit From Bible Study

by Woodrow Kroll

BACK TO THE BIBLE
LINCOLN, NE 68501

17,200 printed to date—1994
(5-9140—17.2M—34)
ISBN 0-8474-0887-6

All Scripture quotations are from
The New King James Version.

Printed in the United States of America.

Introduction

Every Christian knows that to a great extent our spiritual strength is based on our understanding of scripture. We know that the Bible has the answers for life's greatest questions. So why don't we spend more time studying it? Why don't we take what it says more seriously?

Perhaps one of the reasons is that we look at the Bible as unconquerable—too high to climb, like Mount Everest, or too deep to understand, like the depths of the ocean.

The truth is that God gave us His Word as a guide, and He wants us to understand it. It's like a road map. But even road maps need more than a quick glance. If we are to understand a map, we must study it; we must become familiar with what we can learn from it.

That's true of the Bible as well. God wants you to become familiar with His Word. You need to know how you can study it and get something out of it.

Chapter 1

Develop the Right Strategy

Having a strategy is important in everything you do. It keeps you from stumbling through college or business, or even through life.

If you want to be successful in your Bible study, if you want to benefit from it, you must first develop the right strategy.

Here are some things I've learned through decades of Bible study that have helped me develop a workable strategy.

Determine *why* you want to study the Bible

Motive is a key element in how well and how long you will be committed to studying the Bible.

Curiosity is not a good reason to study it. If you are merely curious about what's in the Bible, your curiosity will be satisfied quickly. Then you will likely set it aside, as millions of Christians have already done, and you won't often have the urge to pick it up again.

Looking for mistakes or inaccuracies in the Bible is another insufficient reason to study it. Some people are obsessed with finding so-called discrepancies. Others look for unanswerable questions. Their motive is not to benefit from Bible study; it's to satisfy their need to criticize.

The best way to approach Bible study is with a contemplative look. That's what you need to develop.

Contemplate who wrote the Bible. Come to it with the thirst of the psalmist: "As the deer pants for the water brooks, so pants my soul for You, O God" (Ps. 42:1). Contemplate *why* God wants to speak to you. And contemplate *what* He has to say.

The Bible is the story of God's love for you. When you study it, you will come to know Him better and experience His love more deeply. Look for His love on every page. Make that your strategy, and you'll never be disappointed.

Determine the right approach for you

Once you know what you're looking for in Bible study, decide on an approach.

Should you study alone? If you are very disciplined and study well independently, you may choose this approach.

Should you join a Bible study group or have your family join you in your study? If you find that other people open new ideas to you, study with others. As you listen to them, you may find new horizons opening for you.

You don't have to confine your study to one approach. You can join a Bible study group and at the same time engage in individual Bible study. In fact, that's preferable. You can never learn too much.

There is no right way to study the Bible. There is only a right way for you.

Choose an appropriate time and place to study

Let's say that you choose to study the Bible on your own. How do you get started?

6

I suggest that you don't just jump in. Give some thought to the right time and place for your study. Deciding what is right will be based on many factors. For example, what time of the day are you least apt to be interrupted? Surely it's not when you are getting the kids off to school or preparing supper. Neither is it just after you've come home from the office or in from the fields. Select a better time.

I find that mornings are the best time for me. Mornings have always been the least hectic. Even when my children were growing up, the house was more quiet in the morning than at any other time.

Maybe mornings aren't good for you. No problem. Find a time that is. When you settle on a time, don't change it unless you absolutely have to. You have made an appointment with God and His Word, just as you make appointments in the business world. Is any business appointment more important than an appointment with God? Pick a time and keep it.

Also pick a place. This is more important than you may at first think. The atmosphere, the ambiance of the room, affects your study. If the room is not well lighted, if the furniture is too hard (or too soft), if there is activity nearby, you may be distracted from what God wants you to learn. I never study facing a window; it's too easy to look out and let my mind wander.

Perhaps you will choose to study at the kitchen table. That's not a bad place if you can keep your study materials at hand. That's where you eat physical food. Why not make it the place you eat spiritual food too? Besides, if you miss your Bible study time, you may be reminded of it when you sit down to eat your meals.

7

Set some goals for yourself

I set goals for the year, the month, the week and the day in my study. I want to read through the Bible each year, just as a matter of principle. But I also want to study specific portions of it more deeply each year.

Monthly and weekly goals keep me on course. If it's my goal to learn how God rewards integrity and faithfulness, I may choose to study how He dealt with His servant Job. That's a month-long project. A week-long project may be to compare Job's attitude toward his friends with their attitude toward him. Such a study would teach me about godly attitudes.

When you set goals that cover a whole year, you keep moving in your study. I do not allow myself to get bogged down. If I cannot fully understand something one day, I don't quit. I go on. Perhaps something I study a week later will answer my question.

Set some goals for your study of the Bible. Pace yourself. Know where you want to go and how you will get there. And when you reach your goals, don't forget to thank God for teaching you.

Report what you have learned to someone else

One reason why many Christians are not consistent in their study of the Bible is that they feel that they are making little progress. They study for a week or two, and then they lose interest. It's easy to get discouraged.

But one way for you to beat the Bible study blues is to tell someone else, on a regular basis, what you have learned. This is not a report session as much as it is an opportunity for you to share the joy of learning.

Don't be afraid that you will embarrass yourself. It doesn't matter if the new truth you have discovered is an old truth to your listener. All of us have had to discover those truths at some point in our Christian lives. Your friend should be just as happy that *you* have discovered this truth as he was when *he* discovered it for himself.

If through your Bible study you are blessed with spiritual insight, make sure that you share it. When you report to others what you have learned, you not only share truth but you cement that truth in your mind at the same time.

Bible study is exciting, exhilarating, entertaining and enduring. But it is best accomplished when you develop the right strategy.

Chapter 2

Acquire the Right Tools

Once you have developed a strategy for studying the Word, you may then want to give some thought to acquiring the right tools for your study.

The right tools make a job much easier. I'm not a very good handyman around the house. Oh, I can fix things that get broken. I have remodeled rooms in our house, done landscaping in the yard and things like that. But I don't consider myself a carpenter or a gardener, and I certainly don't consider myself a plumber.

I am, however, a better carpenter when I have the right carpenter's tools. For years I cut two-by-fours with a handsaw, sanded wood surfaces with a piece of sandpaper and swept up the mess with a kitchen broom. But now I have a circular saw, a vibrating sander and a shop broom. Things go much better for me now when household repairs are necessary. What a difference the right tools make!

The same is true when you study the Bible. Some basic tools, as listed in this chapter, will greatly enhance your time in God's Word. You can learn about more tools from your pastor or your local Christian bookstore. New and more user-friendly tools are coming out all the time. But they can't help you unless you know they exist, so keep up on additional tools that can make your Bible study more meaningful.

The following list of basic tools is not exhaustive.

The Bible

The most basic tool of all is the Bible. That may sound obvious, but there are fellow believers in places like China who don't have Bibles. All they have is a few scraps of paper on which some selected verses of the Bible have been written. We should never take our Bibles for granted.

What kind of Bible do you have? Is it one that you are comfortable with? Do you find it readable?

There are many Bibles available today. We have versions, paraphrases, revisions and more. We have study Bibles, parallel text Bibles, reference Bibles and computer Bibles. You can buy a teacher's Bible, a mother's Bible, a student's Bible—almost any kind of Bible you want.

Publishers will publish any kind of Bible you will buy. But never forget: There is a catastrophic chasm between buying a Bible and studying one. If you own one but do not read it, you are like a person who owns an airplane but never flies it.

Decide which Bible is for you. You need not buy a new one to begin your study. One that's older and more a part of you may be even better. It's like an old shoe; you are comfortable with it.

Bible dictionary

A very helpful tool in your study is a Bible dictionary. This differs from an ordinary dictionary in that it defines and describes only those people, places and things mentioned in the Bible.

Why do you need one? For one thing, it will save you a lot of time. You can look up something you don't understand and go right back to your study with greater insight. It can also keep you from confusing or misconstruing people and places.

Here's an example. In Ezra 10 there is a list of priests who had taken pagan wives and were required to divorce them. Ezra 10:21 says that among these priests were the "sons of Harim: Maaseiah, Elijah, Shemaiah, Jehiel, and Uzziah." Are you surprised that Elijah was married to a pagan wife and divorced her? You shouldn't be, but you shouldn't be confused either. This Elijah is not the same as the great prophet who challenged the prophets of Baal on Mount Carmel.

A Bible dictionary will help you distinguish between people and places that have the same name. It will also define words and concepts with which you are unfamiliar.

Many excellent Bible dictionaries are available today. My favorites are *The New Unger's Bible Dictionary*, *The New Bible Dictionary* and one to which I am a contributor, *Nelson's Illustrated Bible Dictionary*.

Bible concordance

A Bible concordance lists every word found in the Bible and every verse in which that word is used. If you have a verse in mind and you don't know where to find it in the Bible, select any word from the verse and look it up in the concordance.

Some concordances can do more. For example, *Strong's Concordance* also features a numbering system that enables you to know the Hebrew or Greek word from which the English word is derived. You don't have to know Hebrew or Greek to use it.

Two other concordances are popular among Bible students—*Young's Concordance* and *Cruden's Concordance.*

Commentaries

Commentaries are very useful tools for the student of the Bible. A commentary contains helpful comments and explanations about a passage of Scripture. Commentaries come in all shapes and sizes. There are one-volume commentaries that say a little something about every book of the Bible, and there are multiple-volume commentaries that are more detailed.

The purposes of commentaries differ widely. Some are critical commentaries, in which the authors spend much of their efforts addressing the original languages of the text. Other commentaries are devotional in nature. Their purpose is to explain the Bible in such a way as to inspire you and move you to greater devotion to God.

Here are some important commentaries: Warren W. Wiersbe's *With the Word Bible Commentary*, a good example of a devotional commentary; John Walvoord's and Roy Zuck's *The Bible Knowledge Commentary*, a complete commentary in two volumes; and William Hendriksen's *New Testament Commentary*, a multiple-volume set that is as thorough as any commentary in print today.

Before you choose a commentary, you should determine your needs. Examine copies and ask questions to be sure that you get the right one for you.

Notebook and pen

Now we come to what I consider the premier Bible study tools—a notebook and a pen.

Most of what I know of the Bible has not come from the study of Hebrew or Greek. It has not come from reading commentaries or Bible dictionaries. Most of what I know has come directly out of my study of the Word. So before I turn to commentaries, dictionaries or concordances, I turn to the Bible and my notebook and pen.

As I study, I jot down things in my notebook that I have learned, things the Holy Spirit teaches me. There is no better teacher of the Bible than the Holy Spirit. "But the Helper, the Holy Spirit, whom the Father will send in My name, He will teach you all things" (John 14:26). The Spirit of God speaks to us when we read God's Word. He teaches us quietly and certainly.

This is a computer age. There is computer software for almost every one of the tools I have mentioned. If you are computer literate, you will likely find help in such software.

But even though I use these computer programs, I still find a spiral notebook and a pen my best study tools. They are inexpensive. They work well. I can use them anywhere I read the Word. Of all your tools for Bible study, your Bible and a notebook and pen may be the best.

The other tools are helpful, but some of the wisest Christians I know don't own them. They own a Bible, and they read it often.

Chapter 3

Employ the Right Study Habits

You are ready to start. You have a Bible in front of you. You know why you want to study it. You've set some goals for your study, and you know exactly what it is you want to get from your time in the Word. You've even gathered some tools for study, including a notebook and pen. You're all set.

Now what do you do? Just jump in? No. That will get you going, but it won't get you where you want to be as a Christian. You need to employ the following study habits to get the most out of your Bible study.

Pray for understanding

Since the Bible is the revelation of the mind of God to the minds of men, it's a good idea to begin by asking God to share His thinking with you. After all, He's the Author of the Book. You want to know what He had in mind when He wrote it. So ask.

Begin with prayer. Simply ask God to touch you with what His Word says, to teach you what it means and to make you a better Christian from your study of the Word. Don't even open your Bible until you have asked the Spirit of God to teach you. The apostle Paul wrote, "But God has revealed them [the things He wants us to know] to us through His Spirit. For the Spirit searches all things, yes, the deep things of God" (1 Cor. 2:10).

It is true that Bible scholars who know the original languages and have spent a lifetime of study in God's Word may have the edge on you when it comes to discerning spiritual truth, but you should never feel left out. You have the same Teacher that they have—the Holy Spirit. All truth ultimately comes from God, and you can understand the deep things of God just like anybody else. But you have to ask Him to teach you. I wouldn't think of beginning my study without asking for God's help. You shouldn't either.

Use your Bible as a study tool

Let's make a crucial distinction. You limit your power and usefulness to the Lord if all you want to do is to study *about* the Bible. You don't want to study *about* anything. You want to study the *Bible*. Don't miss this distinction.

I have very high regard for God's Word. I treat my Bible with the utmost respect. But I don't worship the pages of print or the cowhide cover. I worship the One who gave us the Bible—God.

Some people do not like to write in their Bibles. They think it's disrespectful. I disagree. I think it shows signs of a real desire to know the Author of the Book.

Years ago one of my Bible teachers in college taught me how to mark my Bible in a meaningful way. I have modified his system somewhat, and you will want to find a system that is meaningful to you. I underline the verses that are the most meaningful to me. If verses have similar thoughts and are on the same or facing pages, I draw lines from one to the other. If I am using a study Bible that has center-line references or notes at the bottom of the page, I connect the verse to the note or reference with a straight line. Sometimes I have even used different colors to signify different major doctrines of Scripture.

In essence, I use my Bible, not as a place to read, but as a place to study. I have written notes in the margins. I have recorded whole sermons on a wide-margin Bible. The Bible is not just a source of information. It is a living, breathing Book that should involve us in its pages. If you do not object to writing in your Bible, you can make it far more meaningful for your study.

Don't use your Bible as a living room, saved only for special occasions. Nobody lives there. Use it as a family room, where people are comfortable. Be comfortable with your Bible. Make what God says more meaningful to you by writing meaningful things in it. Use it as a study tool.

Use your notebook in a supporting role

Next to my Bible, the most important tool I have for studying the Word is my notebook. It's not fancy, and it's inexpensive.

I use my computer for writing, for storing important information, even for preparing my radio messages. But I still use a spiral notebook when I study my Bible.

For me, there is nothing quite as meaningful as receiving some insight from the Spirit and jotting it down right away in my notebook. That way I don't forget it.

Each year I try to read through the Bible in a different translation. I begin each year with a new notebook. I make categories of things I've learned from my reading. You might be surprised at what those categories include. They vary from repeated expressions (for example, "The battle is the Lord's") to the "I am" passages of Scripture. I make note of specific doctrines and special verses that are meaningful to me. One year I even made a list of interesting names I found in the Bible (including Joshbekashah, Maher-Shalal-Hash-Baz and Abraham's nephews Huz and Buz).

Can I find some of this information elsewhere? Of course. In fact, I can find just about all of it elsewhere. But when I discover it for myself, it's mine. That's the thrill of Bible study—making your own discoveries. And a notebook and a pen are the best ways to record your discoveries.

Try the "Three M" approach

There are all kinds of ways to study God's Word. You should try several of them to see which one is right for you. I have had great success in what I call the "Three M" approach to study: *meditate, memorize* and *marinate.*

The first *M* is for *meditate.* Reading God's Word is instructive just by itself. But frequently God tells us to meditate on the things we've read. That makes them even more meaningful.

"This Book of the Law shall not depart from your mouth, but you shall meditate in it day and night, that you may observe to do according to all that is written in it. For then you will make your way prosperous, and then you will have good success" (Josh. 1:8).

When you meditate in God's Word, He lays out for you the best possible path for your life. That's what is meant by *good success*. Psalm 1:2 says that the happy man delights "in the Law of the LORD; and in His Law he meditates day and night."

After you have read the passage you want to study, spend a few minutes meditating on it. Ask yourself what God said in it and what He meant by what He said. Ask yourself how it can be meaningful to you. That's meditation.

The second *M* of your Bible study is *memorize*. Commit the verse or passage you're studying to memory so you will always have it with you. You never know when that particular verse is just what you need to make a difference in your life.

The psalmist said, "Your word I have hidden in my heart, that I might not sin against You" (Ps. 119:11).

Memorization makes the Word permanent in your heart and mind. "I will delight myself in Your statutes; I will not forget Your word" (Ps. 119:16). When you memorize Scripture, your heart is enriched and your mind is challenged for more than just a moment.

The final *M* in the Three M approach is *marinate*. When you marinate meat, you soak it in a savory sauce or solution. The meat soaks up the spices, and it is both enriched and tenderized. That's a wonderful

21

picture of what should happen to our minds when we spend time in God's Word. When we spend enough time in God's Word, we allow it to marinate our minds, to tenderize them, to cause them to soak up the herbs and spices of God's truth.

If we meditate, memorize and marinate, we cannot rush to the study of the Word and rush away from it. All three take time, and so does effective Bible study. Set aside the time. Make the commitment. Try the Three M approach in your study of the Word.

Check your understanding with others

It's exciting to make a private discovery of God's truth. You are amazed at what you have learned. But it's a good idea to check your understanding with others who have been studying the Word for a few years. This is the time to read the commentaries to see if the "experts" agree with you. This is the time to run something by your pastor to make sure your understanding is correct. This is the time to share your insight with someone older and wiser in the faith.

I have a dear friend who is a wonderful Bible student, but he is entirely self-taught. While he has a good grasp of fundamental truth in God's Word, he also has some of the wackiest ideas I have ever heard. Why? Because he has never checked his own conclusions with those who know what is true.

When you commit yourself to serious study of the Bible, make sure you employ the right study habits, and be sure to share your conclusions with others who can affirm them or help you correct them. After all, the Spirit of God may be your Teacher, but He is the Teacher of others also. None of us has a private lock on the truth. We need to submit our conclusions to the scrutiny of others. That's a good study habit to get into.

Chapter 4

Make the Right Use of What You Learn

What are your reasons for studying God's Word? Do you want to better understand what the Bible is all about? Do you want to know more about God? Obviously there are many reasons for studying the Bible. Some are good, and some are not so good.

Sometimes our motivation in Bible study is simply to get a good grasp of the facts. We want to impress everyone in our Bible study groups with what we know. But that's study for the sake of pride, and God hates pride (Prov. 8:13). At other times we may study the Bible out of guilt. We feel that Bible study is something we *must* do to be spiritual; and like it or not, we have to do it.

We can be wrong in our motivation for studying the Scriptures, and we can also be wrong in the way we use the Scriptural knowledge after we gain it.

What use will you make of your study of the Word? What outcome do you want to see from all the time you'll spend in study? Think about this before you begin. Here are some outcomes worthy of your effort.

Study the Bible to please God

Everyone wants to please those whom he respects. We work hard to please our supervisors. We study hard in college to please our parents and professors. But whom should we want to please more than God? Whom should the Christian regard more highly than Him?

Wasn't the goal of the Lord Jesus to please His Father? He said, "When you lift up the Son of Man, then you will know that I am He, and that I do nothing of Myself; but as My Father taught Me, I speak these things. . . . For I always do those things that please Him" (John 8:28–29).

Jesus knew that reading the Word pleased His Father. He disputed the meaning of it with the teachers in the temple. And when His father and mother returned to Jerusalem, anxiously looking for Him, Jesus responded, "Did you not know that I must be about My Father's business?" (Luke 2:49). The study of God's Word is God's business. We need to get to it!

The psalmist saw the connection between Bible study and pleasing God when he prayed, "Deal bountifully with Your servant, that I may live and keep Your word. Open my eyes, that I may see wondrous things from Your Law" (Ps. 119:17–18).

One of the major outcomes we seek from the study of God's Word is simply to please God. That's reason enough to spend time in it—but there's more.

Study the Bible for spiritual growth

Bible study pleases God and strengthens us. We are twice benefited from those golden moments in His Word.

A systematic study of it (setting aside a time and a place every day to do some meaningful study) is the engine that drives spiritual growth. The believer would be stuck in spiritual infancy if it were not for God's Word. Only when we move away from the milk of the Word to its meat do we begin to grow strong spiritual bones and muscles.

The Bible is the food for our spiritual nourishment (1 Pet. 2:2). It is the spiritual lamp to guide us as we walk through a minefield of temptations (Ps. 119:105). It is also the primary weapon in our spiritual warfare with Satan (Eph. 6:17). The Bible is like a Swiss army knife—everything we need is in it. It is our equipment for every good work (2 Tim. 3:17).

How are you doing in your spiritual growth? Have you grown deeper, broader, higher, richer in the Word during the last year? Has your knowledge of the Word grown in any significant degree? Are you grappling with the serious questions of doctrine? Or are you still trying to memorize John 3:16?

Vance Havner, the country preacher, once told me that how long we have been saved tells us only how long we've been on the road. It doesn't tell us how far we've come. How true! Many Christians have been on the road for years, but they have spent so little time in Bible study that they haven't come very far. They are still spiritual pygmies, when they could be spiritual giants.

Don't let that happen to you. Begin a regular study of God's Word. Stay in it. As you study, you will please God, and you will also prepare yourself for spiritual growth.

Study the Bible to be a fit defender of the faith

If you read, memorize and understand the Word, you become a prime candidate for being used by God to defend the faith. You'll be much more than "the answer man." You'll be respected for the knowledge God has given you, and you will likely be called on when matters of faith are in question.

When this happens, never speak as an "authority," but rather as a meek "student." Remember Peter's admonition to the Bible students of his day: "Sanctify the Lord God in your hearts, and always be ready to give a defense to everyone who asks you a reason for the hope that is in you, with meekness and fear" (1 Pet. 3:15).

Don't be proud of your knowledge of the Bible. It comes by God's grace just like any other gift. He's the One who gives you understanding. He is your Teacher; you are the pupil.

Unsaved people don't want to hear Christians talking about salvation when we don't have answers to their basic questions. They are tired of listening to people who don't know what they're talking about. We must be students of the Word. We must be able to defend what we believe. Cult members easily defend what they believe. Should we be any less prepared?

Study the Bible to tell others about Christ

In football, defense is only half the team. The other half is offense. We need to do more than defend the faith. We need to study the Bible so we can become equipped to tell others about God's great love for them and Christ's great sacrifice at Calvary.

God has used me to lead hundreds of people to Himself, but I don't think I've ever said the same thing to any two of them. When I talk to them about their salvation, I have no set formula, no memorized

28

speech. Of course, there are certain facts I must include in our conversation, and there are certain verses that lend themselves well to getting those facts across. It is extremely important in personal evangelism to know the Word well enough to tell others about Christ without fear.

If you find it difficult to share your faith, it's likely that you suffer from one of two concerns. You are embarrassed to talk about religious things, or you fear that the person will ask you a question you can't answer.

I can't answer all their questions either. But the more I study God's Word, the bolder I become in my personal witness for the Lord. One of the wonderful results of Bible study is being set free from the fear of being stumped over some Bible question. Let God take the fear away; replace it with a sure and certain knowledge of His Word. You'll be surprised how much more confident you will be.

Study the Bible to teach others about God

It's important to tell others about Christ. We are saved because someone told us about Him. But we must also be able to teach others about God. Your ability to teach is based largely on your understanding of the Bible. And your understanding is based on how effective your study of the Word has been.

Teachers may be born, but they are not born with knowledge. That comes through diligent study. You may be a born teacher, but you must acquire the knowledge of God in order to teach the Word of God. Paul taught Timothy the Word and then encouraged him. He said, "The things that you have heard from me among many witnesses, commit these things to faithful men who will be able to teach others also" (2 Tim. 2:2).

We must never study the Bible for the purpose of becoming Bible students or renowned scholars. We study it with the purpose that lives will be changed—our own and those of the people God calls us to minister to.

God wrote only one Bible. How much do you know about it? How well have you mastered it? Has your knowledge resulted in personal spiritual growth? Is God pleased with your knowledge of His Word?

Back to the Bible is a nonprofit ministry dedicated to Bible teaching, evangelism and edification of Christians worldwide.

If we may assist you in knowing more about Christ and the Christian life, please write to us without obligation.

Back to the Bible
P.O. Box 82808
Lincoln, NE 68501